HYPERSPACE!

Facts and Fun
From All Over
the Universe

HYPERSPACE!

FACTS AND FUN FROM ALL OVER THE UNIVERSE

BY DAVID A. ADLER

Illustrated by FRED WINKOWSKI

The Viking Press, New York

First Edition
Text Copyright © 1982 by David A. Adler
Illustrations Copyright © 1982 by Fred Winkowski
All rights reserved
First published in 1982 in simultaneous hardcover and paperback editions
by The Viking Press, 625 Madison Avenue, New York, New York 10022
Published simultaneously in Canada by Penguin Books Canada Limited
Printed in U.S.A.
1 2 3 4 5 86 85 84 83 82

Library of Congress Cataloging in Publication Data
Adler, David A. Hyperspace!: facts and fun from all over the universe.
Summary: Includes facts, puzzles, riddles, brain teasers, and games
about the sun, stars, planets, and other aspects of outer space.
1. Astronomy—Juvenile literature. [1. Astronomy.
2. Scientific recreations] I. Winkowski, Fred, ill.   II. Title.
QB46.A34   520   81–70404 (hardcover and paperback)
ISBN 0–670–38908–0 (hardcover)   AACR2
ISBN 0–670–05117–9 (paperback)

To my cousins,
Nathan, Jonathan,
Joshua, and Raphael
D. A. A.

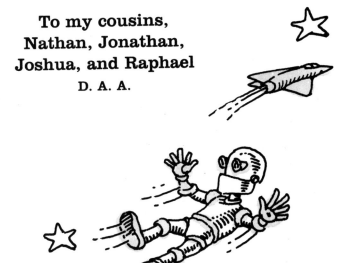

To my mother and father
F. W.

CONTENTS

HYPERSPACE!

Facts and Fun

From All Over

the Universe

THE SUN IS A STAR

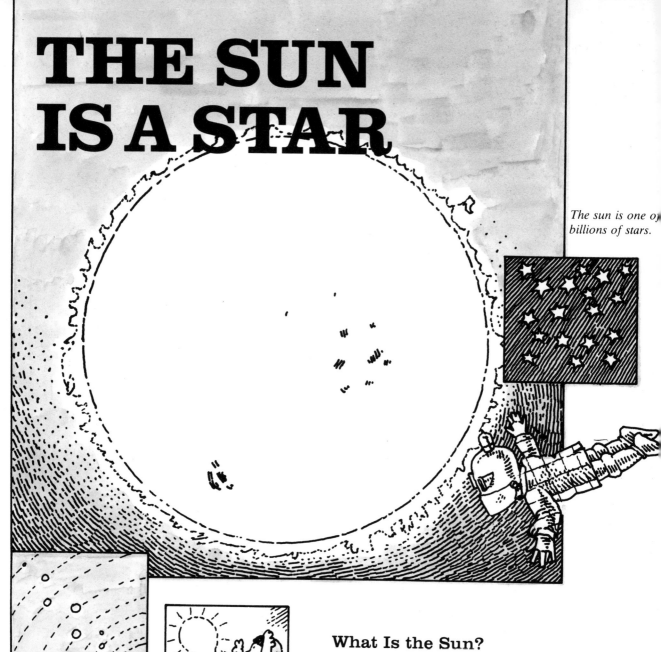

The sun is one of billions of stars.

The sun is the source of our heat and light.

What Is the Sun?

The sun is a star, one of billions of stars. It is the star closest to Earth.

The sun is a huge ball of gas. It's the center of the solar system. The sun's gravity holds Earth and the other planets in their orbits.

The sun is the source of our heat, our light, our wind and rain. The sun is the source of all life on Earth.

The Sun Is Big, and It's Hot.

The sun's diameter is about one hundred times as big as Earth's. How big is that? Imagine the Earth to be as small as a Ping-Pong ball; then the sun would be a huge ball more than twice the size of an average adult.

The sun's surface is some 10,000 degrees Fahrenheit. That's about 5600 degrees Celsius. If a spaceship landed on the sun, it would burn instantly. Deep inside the sun it's even hotter, millions of degrees hotter.

Imagine Earth as small as a Ping-Pong ball.

FLY TOO CLOSE TO THE SUN AGAIN? DID YOU, JOHNSON?

If You Stood on the Sun . . .

Of course you can't stand on the sun. It's much too hot. But if you could, what would Earth look like from so far away? The sun is about 93 million miles away. That's about 150 million kilometers.

To get an idea of how far away that is, drop a Ping-Pong ball at one end of a large open field. Then walk away from the ball. Walk in a straight line and take 475 steps. Then turn around and look at the ball. Does it look small? That's how Earth would look to you if you were standing on the sun.

475 STEPS

What Makes the Sun So Hot?

The sun is made up of many elements; mostly it is a huge ball of hot, dense hydrogen and helium gas. Tiny particles of these gases are moving at very high speeds. When they crash, some of the hydrogen atoms change to helium. This is the same kind of change that causes a hydrogen bomb to explode. On the sun these explosions are happening all the time. And, just like a bomb, the sun gives off a tremendous amount of heat and light.

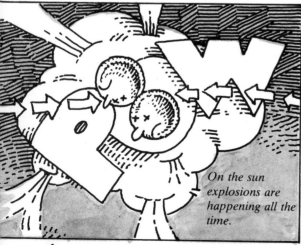

On the sun explosions are happening all the time.

4

Sun Power

The sun keeps us warm. Even on a cold winter day the sun warms us. The fossil fuels we burn in our heaters—the coal, oil, and natural gas—come from plants and animals that lived ages ago. The plants stored the sun's energy, and the animals ate the plants. When we burn fossil fuels, we are releasing that solar energy. The sun's energy in fossil fuels also powers our cars, trains, and factories.

The sun also causes wind and rain, which turn windmills and water mills to give us power.

Scientists have tried for many years to make direct use of the sun's energy. But it is not easy. While a huge amount of energy reaches Earth each day, it is spread out. The amount of sunlight reaching any one spot is small. One method of collecting the sun's energy uses black panels that absorb the sun's light and heat. Behind the panels is water in glass tubes. The water is heated and can then be circulated through a radiator to heat a home.

Warning: The Sun's Light Can Be Dangerous!

Never look straight at the sun, not even if you're wearing sunglasses, and certainly not through a telescope or binoculars. The sun's light is very strong and can damage your eyes. It can even cause blindness.

Sunlight also affects your skin. It can give you a tan, but too much sun can dry your skin and give it a leathery look. Too much sun can even cause skin cancer.

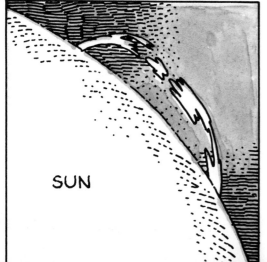

The Sun Moves, Too.

The sun spins around its own axis. It takes about a month for the sun to make one complete turn. Since the sun is a ball of gas, all parts don't move at the same speed. The gases around the sun's middle, its equator, make the turn in slightly less than a month.

The sun also travels around the center of its family of stars, the Milky Way Galaxy. Scientists estimate it will take 225 million years to complete this trip around the galaxy.

Sunspots

Sunspots are areas on the sun which, from Earth, look like dark spots or holes. They're about 8000 degrees Fahrenheit, which is about 4500 degrees Celsius. That's hotter than any fire on Earth. Sunspots look dark to us on Earth because they're areas that are not as hot as the rest of the sun. Sunspots can be many times bigger than Earth, and they usually last only about a week.

Sunspots near the center of the sun move faster than those at the top or bottom. This proved to scientists that the sun is not solid; it is a huge spinning ball of gas.

Prominences

Sometimes huge streams of glowing gas, called prominences, leap up from the sun. They can leap as high as 20,000 miles, or about 32,000 kilometers. That's more than double the diameter of Earth! Some prominences last just a few hours; others last as long as a few months.

TRIANGLE PUZZLE

How many triangles are there in this drawing of the sun?

Answer on page 71.

Which is heavier, the sun or the moon?
The moon. The sun is very light.

Why was the sun on TV?
Because it's a star.

If a rooster laid an egg on the sun, would it hatch?
Roosters don't lay eggs.

Why was the silly astronomer looking for a switch?
He wanted to turn on the sky light.

When is the sun yellow on the outside and red on the inside?
When it swallows a cherry.

What's black and yellow, black and yellow, black and yellow?
The sun in a tuxedo rolling down a hill.

What's yellow, brown, and mushy?
A rotten sun.

RIDDLES

Which two of these suns are exactly the same?

1

2

3

4

5

6

What's the difference between the sun and a jazz musician?
One keeps us hot. The other keeps us cool.

How are the sun and a frightened sailor the same?
They're both yellow.

What's lighter than the sun?
A feather.

Why did the silly astronomer's house collapse?
He built it with sunbeams.

Find three numbers that add up to exactly 100. Use only the numbers on the rays of this sun, and don't use any number more than once.

28 51 62 13 24 39 58 47 71 37

Answers on page 71.

9

SUN WORDS

Here are some
sun words and expressions:
Can you tell what they are?
Answers on next page.

Can you escape the sun's pull of gravity without crossing any lines?
Use your finger to trace a path away from the sun.
Answer on page 71.

Answers:
1. A sunburst
2. A sunset
3. Father and sun
4. Sunglasses
5. A sunbird
6. A sunbonnet
7. Sunlight

THE EARTH: A Big, Round, Solid Ball

Earth is home for four and a half billion people.

What Is Earth?

Earth is a big, round, solid ball of stone and metal covered with water, rocks, and dirt. It is a planet, one of nine planets that rotate around the sun. Earth is a huge magnet with two poles, the North Pole and the South Pole. It is home for four and a half billion people.

Day and Night

If you think you see the sun rising each morning, your eyes are fooling you. The sun is not rising at all. It stays pretty still in relation to Earth. It is Earth that is moving.

Day and night are caused by the spinning of Earth. As it spins, one half is moving toward the sun's light. For people living on that half, it is morning; to them, it seems that the sun is rising. As one half of the Earth is spinning toward the light, the other half is spinning away from it. For people living on that half, night is coming and it seems that the sun is setting.

PROJECT: Earth Moves, Moves, Moves.

A spinning top can help you to understand how Earth moves in three different ways.

Take a top and spin it. When the top spins, it spins on its own axis, an imaginary line that runs through the center of the top. Earth moves in the same way as it spins on its own axis. It makes one complete turn each day.

You can see that the spinning top doesn't stay in one place as it spins. It moves in a winding circular pattern. Earth also moves as it spins. It moves in an orbit around the sun. It makes one trip every 365¼ days.

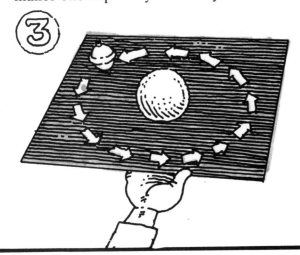

If you spin the top on a large piece of cardboard, it will help you to understand how Earth moves as part of the Milky Way Galaxy. While the top is spinning, move the cardboard. Now the top is moving three ways. It's spinning, moving in a winding, circular pattern, and the cardboard it's spinning on is moving, too. While Earth is spinning on its own axis and rotating around the sun, the Milky Way is moving, too. And as the galaxy moves, so does everything in it, including Earth.

Our Seasons

Our four seasons are made by sunshine, the movement of Earth around the sun, and the tilt of Earth.

Earth is a cold place. All its light and heat come from the sun. During the summer, because Earth is tilted, we get more sunshine, more light and heat than we get in winter. But while we're getting more than twelve hours of sunshine a day in the Northern Hemisphere, the Southern Hemisphere is getting less than twelve hours of sunshine. That's why, when it is summer for us, it is winter in the Southern Hemisphere.

PROJECT: More Sun in the Summer and Less Sun in the Winter

To understand how, as Earth turns, half of Earth can get more than half a day of sunshine, take a flashlight and a ball. If the ball does not have a seam, draw a line around its middle. Turn on the flashlight and let it rest on a table. Darken the room. Then hold the ball so the light from the flashlight shines on it. Now

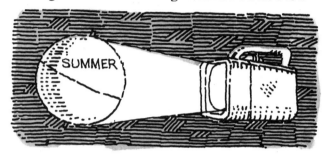

tilt the ball so the line is not perfectly horizontal. As you turn the ball, you will see that one half of the ball gets more light than the other half. That's what happens on Earth. The half of Earth getting more than half a day of sunshine is having summer. As Earth

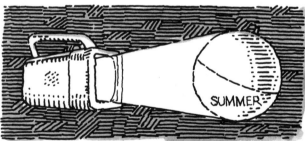

travels around the sun, the amount of sunshine each half of Earth gets keeps changing. Earth revolves around the sun once each year, making one full cycle of seasons.

What's Between Earth and Outer Space?

If you jump, you don't jump into outer space. You jump into the atmosphere. It is between Earth and outer space.

Our atmosphere is made up of gases, water vapor, and tiny particles too small to be seen. The atmosphere closest to Earth—the air we breathe—is mostly nitrogen (78%) and oxygen (21%). Other gases, including helium, carbon dioxide, and argon, make up the other 1% of the air.

Earth's atmosphere does not go on forever. The farther from Earth you travel, the thinner the atmosphere gets until at some point, a few hundred miles up, the atmosphere fades and outer space begins.

If You Dig a Hole That's Really Deep . . .

Earth is a big, round, solid ball. But while Earth is solid, it is not the same all the way through.

The outer layer of Earth is called the crust. It is the part we live on, dig into, and when we crawl into a cave, it's the part we explore. Beneath the crust is Earth's mantle. Beneath the mantle, at the very center of Earth, is its core.

Earth's crust is made of rock. It is about twenty-two miles, or thirty-five kilometers, deep under land, and about three miles, or five kilometers, deep under parts of the ocean. Twenty-two miles might seem quite deep, but it isn't really. If you were to dig a hole through the center of Earth, you would have to dig almost 12,500 kilometers before you came out the other end. That's more than eight thousand miles!

No one has ever dug beneath Earth's crust. But scientists have some clues about what lies below. Volcanic lava has come up from the mantle. And because vibrations travel at different speeds through different kinds of rock, scientists have studied the vibrations caused by earthquakes for clues about Earth's mantle. Scientists believe that the various parts of the solar system have many things in common, so meteorites that have fallen to Earth have left clues, too.

What lies below Earth's mantle? Earth's core. It is made of rock and metal. The deeper you go, the hotter it gets. In the inner core, the deepest part of Earth, scientists believe that the metal there, probably iron, is some 9000 degrees Fahrenheit. That's about 5000 degrees Celsius—and that's hot!

Imagine Earth with No Force of Gravity.

Gravity is the pulling force that gives us weight. Since Earth is always spinning, without gravity we would all fly off into space. Cars, buildings, and the water that fills our oceans would fly off, too. That won't happen, though, because Earth's gravity is here to stay.

Earth is not the only thing that has gravity. Even a small stone has some. Of course, the strength of the stone's pull of gravity is very slight. The strength of an object's pull of gravity is based on its mass. Earth has greater mass than the moon, so its pull of gravity is stronger. The sun's pull is stronger than Earth's. The sun's powerful pull of gravity keeps all the planets of the solar system in their orbits.

Earth Surprises

Earth is mostly wet. If you look at a globe, you will notice that most of Earth, about 70%, is covered with water.

Earth is not perfectly round. It is somewhat flat at the North and South poles. And while the equator is the imaginary line around Earth's middle, it is not Earth's fattest part. Earth is fattest just below the equator.

How much you weigh depends on where you are. On Earth you don't always weigh the same. Because the pull of gravity is strongest when you are closest to Earth, you weigh slightly more at sea level than you do while standing on the top of a high mountain.

16

START

Use your finger to find
a path back to Earth without
touching a star.

Answer on page 71.

17

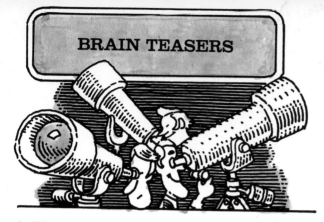

BRAIN TEASERS

1. Three astronomers, Joseph, Edward, and Nathan, were at a world conference. One of the three came from Canada. One came from the United States, and one came from Australia. Read the statements below and decide who came from where.

  a. A small delegation came from Canada.
  b. Nathan is wearing a brown suit.
  c. Nathan is either from Canada or Australia.
  d. Joseph is part of a large delegation.
  e. The Canadian delegates are all wearing green pants.

2. If a jet circles the earth at 500 mph for half its way around Earth and at 1,000 mph for the other half, what is its average speed?

3. If one jet can travel around the world in six days and a second jet can make the trip in three days and they start from the same place and fly in opposite directions, after how many days will they pass each other?

4. A tall man on a street corner was selling Earth. A bald man came by and bought Earth for a dollar. "Why did you buy it?" his brother asked. "I bought it because I can sell it for more," the bald man told his brother.

The bald man and his brother stood on the corner and sold Earth. They sold it to the tall man for ten dollars.

The tall man bought Earth so he could sell it again. And he did. He sold it to the bald man and his brother for twenty dollars.

The bald man and his brother stood on the corner and tried to sell Earth. No one wanted it. So the bald man told the tall man, "We're having a sale. We'll sell you Earth for just fifteen dollars. That's less than we paid for it. If you're smart you'll buy it so you can sell it again."

The tall man paid the fifteen dollars and bought back Earth. Then he tried to sell it to the bald man and his brother. But the bald man wouldn't buy it. "Only a fool," he said, "would buy Earth from a man on a corner."

Who was the fool? After all that buying and selling, who lost money and how much?

Answers on page 71.

18

RIDDLES

What on Earth is yellow and fast?
A jet-propelled banana.

What on Earth is purple and dangles?
A grape earring.

What on Earth is tall and red?
A strawberry in high heels.

Where on Earth would you
find green pigs?
Just where you left them.

Who's big and round
and thinks you're
cute?
Aunt Earthel.

What on Earth is green and giggles?
A ticklish frog.

What on Earth is orange and bowls?
An athletic carrot.

What on Earth is brown on the outside and
purple on the inside?
Buried grapes.

What on Earth is brown on the outside and
brown on the inside?
Buried raisins.

What's round, mostly wet, and goes, "Pop,
chew, chew, pop, chew, chew, pop"?
Earth chewing bubble gum.

19

Hidden Places on Earth

Here's an example of how a place can be hidden in a sentence:

> The artist waS PAINting the king when the king told him to paint a canvas instead.

Now can you find the places hidden in the sentences below?

1. Search in a gift shop and you'll find this country.
2. You'll agree, certainly, that this country is slippery.
3. "I am Eric," a little boy said. "Can you guess where I live?"
4. Carla then set sail for this city by the sea.

Answers: 1. China. 2. Greece. 3. America. 4. Athens.

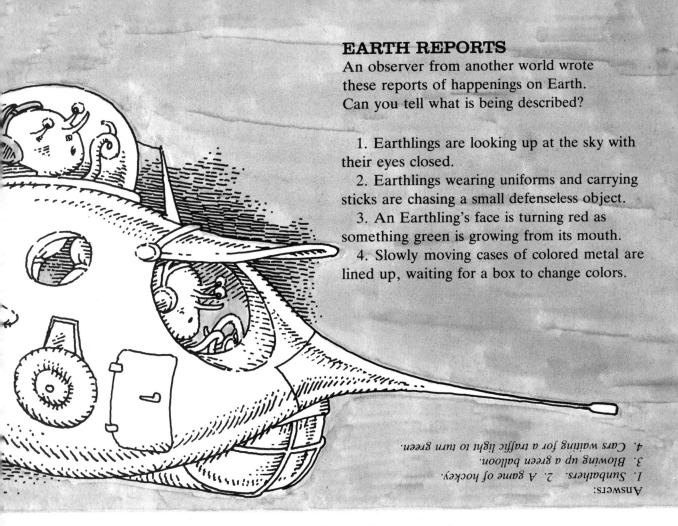

EARTH REPORTS

An observer from another world wrote
these reports of happenings on Earth.
Can you tell what is being described?

1. Earthlings are looking up at the sky with
their eyes closed.

2. Earthlings wearing uniforms and carrying
sticks are chasing a small defenseless object.

3. An Earthling's face is turning red as
something green is growing from its mouth.

4. Slowly moving cases of colored metal are
lined up, waiting for a box to change colors.

Answers:
1. Sunbathers. 2. A game of hockey.
3. Blowing up a green balloon.
4. Cars waiting for a traffic light to turn green.

AN ART PROJECT: Scratchboard Drawing

If you stand outside on a clear night and
look up at the sky, it will look like a dark sea
of color with dots of light. Here's a fun way to
draw the night sky:

You'll need a small piece of uncoated
cardboard, a black crayon, and a few crayons in
light colors.

First cover one side of the cardboard with
sections of color, using only the light-colored
crayons.

Then, with the black crayon, color over the
other colors so that the only color you see is the
black. Your drawing now looks like the sky
on a stormy night.

With a sharp pencil draw on the black the
stars, planets, and the moon. As you draw,
you are scratching away the black so that the
colors beneath show through.

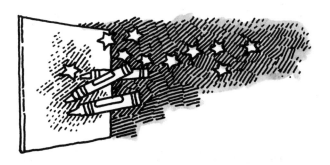

THE MOON IS A ROCK

What Is the Moon?

The moon is a rock, a big rock. Its diameter is 2,160 miles. That is almost 3,500 kilometers. That's about the same as the distance between Chicago and San Francisco. The moon is a satellite of Earth. That means it travels in an orbit, or path, around Earth.

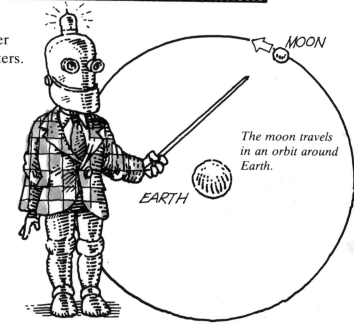

The moon travels in an orbit around Earth.

MOON

EARTH

Compare the diameter of the moon with the size of the United States.

22

How Far Away Is the Moon?

The moon is Earth's closest neighbor in space, but it isn't really very close. The orbit the moon makes around Earth is not perfectly round, so the moon is not always the same distance away. When it is closest to Earth, it is about 221,000 miles away. That's about 350,000 kilometers, which is about nine times the distance around Earth. The farthest away the moon gets is about 252,000 miles, or 400,000 kilometers, away.

The Moon Keeps Moving.

Earth keeps moving, and so does the moon. It travels at a speed of 2,280 miles an hour. That's more than 3,600 kilometers an hour—as fast as the world's fastest jets. The moon circles Earth about once every twenty-seven days. While the moon is traveling around Earth, it is also rotating on its own axis. Each time it circles Earth, it makes one revolution on its axis.

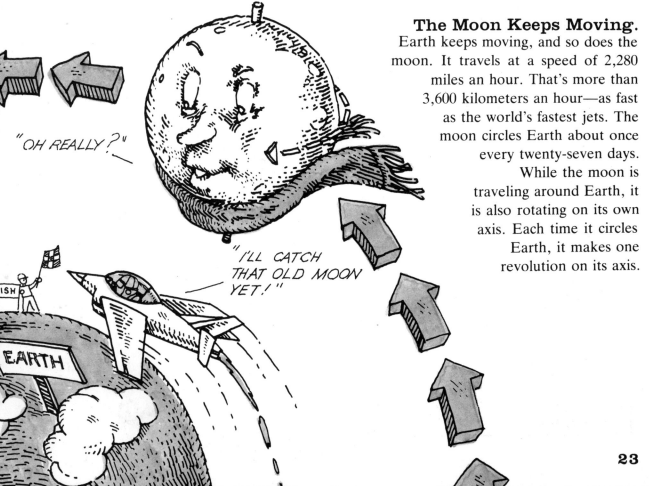

Sometimes It Looks Round.
Sometimes It's a Crescent.
And Sometimes You Can't See the Moon at All.

As the moon travels around Earth, its shape seems to change. Sometimes it looks like a bright globe. At other times it looks like only half a globe, or like a crescent, or it may not be visible at all. But the moon doesn't change. It only seems different to us because the moon has no light of its own. It reflects the sun's light.

PROJECT: Why the Moon Seems to Disappear

If at night you turn off all the lights in your room except one and hold up a large ball, it will help you to understand why the moon looks different to us at different times of the month. The light shines on only half of the ball, the half facing it. The other half is dark.

In the same way, the sun's light shines on only half of the moon.

As the moon circles Earth, sometimes the half facing Earth is also facing the sun. We call that a full moon. When we see only part of the moon, it's because only a part of the lighted half of the moon is facing earth. At the time of the month we call the new moon, we don't see the moon at all because the side facing us is the moon's dark side.

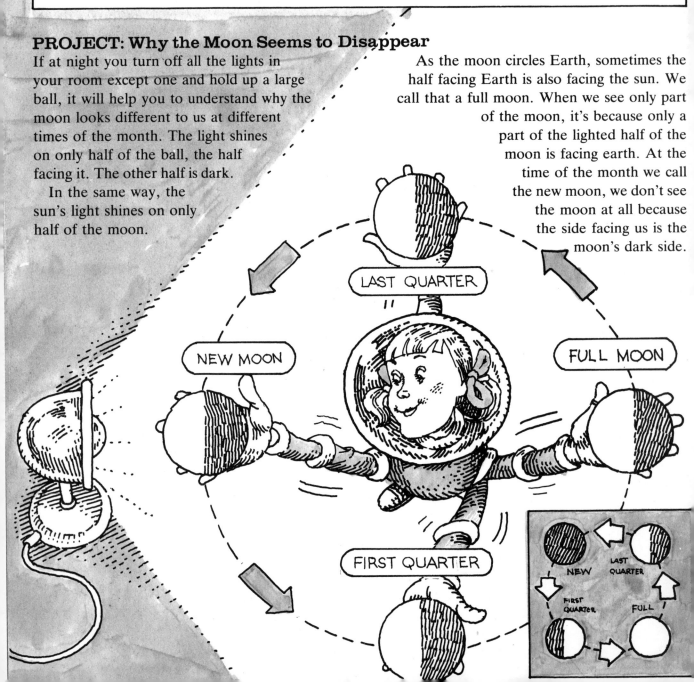

LAST QUARTER

NEW MOON

FULL MOON

FIRST QUARTER

NEW · LAST QUARTER · FIRST QUARTER · FULL

The Moon Is Very, Very Hot and Very, Very Cold.

The sun doesn't always shine on the same side of the moon. As the moon circles Earth, the moon revolves on its own axis. As it turns, any one spot on the moon is dark for two weeks and then light for two weeks. When the moon is dark, it gets colder than 250 degrees below zero Fahrenheit. That is 150 degrees below zero Celsius and much colder than it ever gets on Earth. Where the moon is light, it gets hotter than 250 degrees above zero Fahrenheit, or 120 degrees Celsius. That's so hot you could boil water or cook eggs, spaghetti, or soup without using a stove!

On the Moon There Is No Wind, No Sound, No Rain, No Life.

It isn't only the extreme temperatures on the moon that make it very different from Earth. There is no air or water on the moon. Without air, there can be no wind or sound; without water, there is no rain and no life.

The moon is also much smaller than Earth, so its pull of gravity is less. A person weighing 180 pounds on Earth would weigh only 30 pounds on the moon. And because the pull of gravity is less on the moon, with the same effort it takes you to jump one foot off the ground on Earth, you would jump six feet on the moon. Of course, on the moon, you would have to carry your own air and water supply. You would have to wear a bulky space suit to protect you from the extreme cold or heat. With all that equipment, you might find it difficult to jump.

25

THE WHAT'S THIS
MOON QUIZ

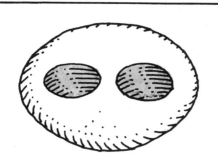

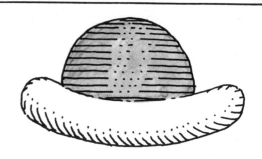

1. What's This?

    a. The moon wearing sunglasses.
    b. Two eggs sunny-side up.
    c. A fat finger bowling ball.

2. What's This?

    a. The moon rising over a frankfurter.
    b. A very fat banana.

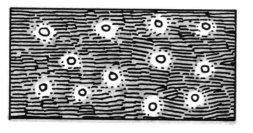

3. What's This?

    a. A warehouse of extra moons.
    b. An aerial photograph of bald men.
    c. A marble convention.
    d. Freckles.

4. What's This?

    a. A squashed moon.
    b. A running ghost.
    c. A lumpy balloon.

5. How Many Astronauts Are Standing on the Moon?

Answers: 1–4. You've probably already guessed that the questions in this quiz are really riddles. Any answer you chose is correct. 5. Nine. Don't tell me you counted the ones lying down!

26

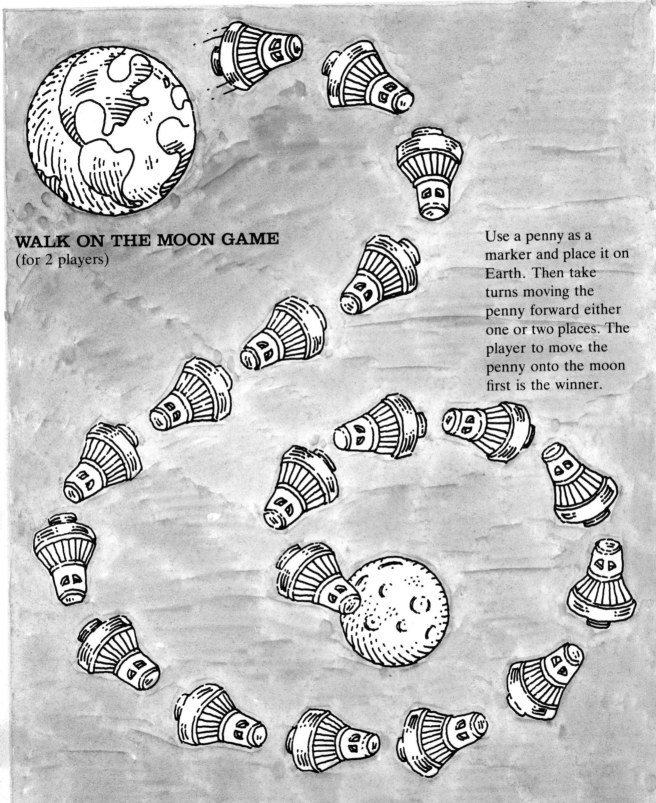

WALK ON THE MOON GAME
(for 2 players)

Use a penny as a marker and place it on Earth. Then take turns moving the penny forward either one or two places. The player to move the penny onto the moon first is the winner.

Astronauts on the Moon

On July 20, 1969, two American astronauts, Neil Armstrong and Edwin Aldrin, became the first people to walk on the moon. When they looked up into space, they saw Earth. The ground the astronauts were walking on was brownish-gray. It was made up of crushed rock and glass. Astronauts Armstrong and Aldrin collected more than forty pounds of soil and rocks from the moon's surface and brought them back to Earth. Some of these rocks

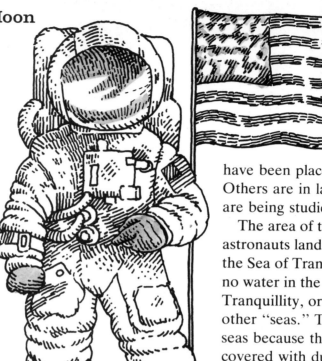

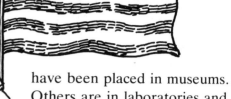

have been placed in museums. Others are in laboratories and are being studied by scientists.

The area of the moon the astronauts landed on is called the Sea of Tranquillity. There is no water in the Sea of Tranquillity, or in the moon's other "seas." They are called seas because they are flat and covered with dust, and from Earth those large flat areas look like huge pools of water, but they are perfectly dry.

Other Moons

Earth's moon is not the only moon in the solar system. Mars has two moons, Phobos and Deimos. They are both much smaller than Earth's moon, and they are much closer to Mars than our moon is to Earth. Some of the other planets also have moons. Neptune has two moons. Uranus has five. Saturn has ten, and Jupiter has at least thirteen moons. All these moons, including Earth's, are natural satellites. Each one revolves around its planet. It is the planet's gravitational pull that keeps a moon from flying off into space.

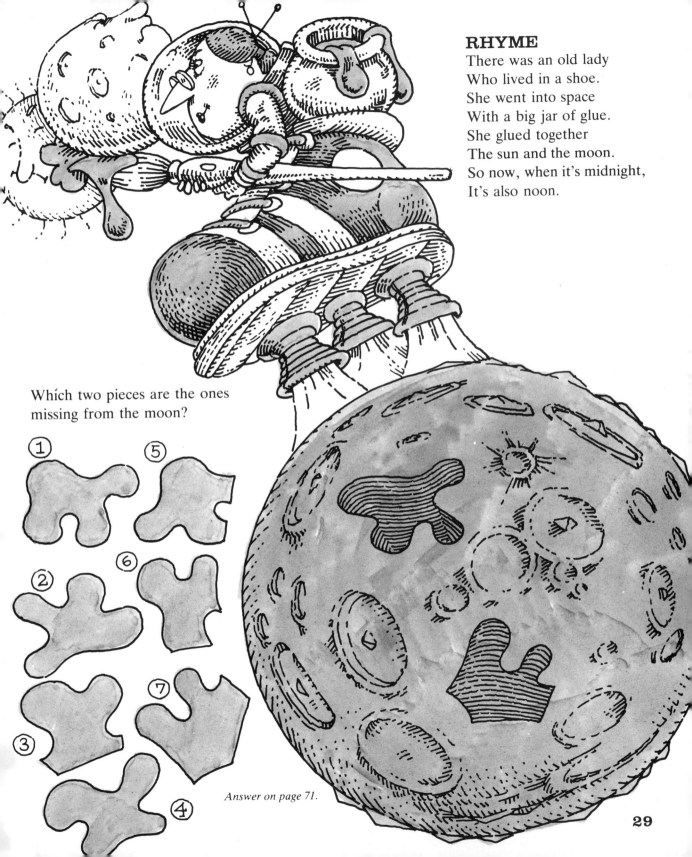

RHYME

There was an old lady
Who lived in a shoe.
She went into space
With a big jar of glue.
She glued together
The sun and the moon.
So now, when it's midnight,
It's also noon.

Which two pieces are the ones missing from the moon?

① ⑤ ② ⑥ ③ ⑦ ④

Answer on page 71.

This picture story of a voyage to the moon is all mixed-up. Can you put these pictures in order?

A

B

C

D

E

F

What is big and round with red and white stripes?

> *A peppermint moon.*

What is big and round, has red and white stripes, and is very sticky?

> *A peppermint moon that's been licked.*

Why is the moon so white?
It brushes after every meal.

On the moon how do you know when it's night?

> *The best TV shows come on.*

RIDDLES

When does the moon stop eating?

When it's full.

Why isn't the moon plugged in?

Because it's battery operated.

Why is it so expensive to buy a moon?

The batteries are not included.

What is white and round and green all over?

A moldy moon.

What is white and round and black and blue?

A bruised moon.

Where are Boardwalk, Park Place, and the Sea of Tranquillity?

In the game of Moonopoly.

What is small and round and covered with ketchup?

A hamburger.

What is big and round and covered with ketchup?

A moonburger.

What are baby moons called?

Golf balls.

If you saved a ball of string as big as the moon, what would you have?

No place to keep it.

Why can't you put out a fire on the moon?

Because you're not there.

Compare the size of these planets.

The planets in the solar system orbit the sun in this order: Mercury, Venus, Earth, Mars, Jupiter, Saturn, Uranus, Neptune, Pluto.

ALL THOSE PLANETS

What Is Mercury?

It is a hot, small, dark, fast-moving planet.

Mercury is the closest planet to the sun. That explains why it is so hot. It is hot enough to melt some metals. And it's perfectly dry.

Mercury is the second smallest planet in the solar system. Its diameter is less than half that of Earth. Mercury is so small that its gravitational pull is not very strong. It is not even strong enough to hold onto its own atmosphere. Without an atmosphere, there is nothing above the surface of Mercury to reflect the sun's light. That's why Mercury is dark.

Mercury has to move fast to escape the sun's powerful gravitational pull. Mercury

Mercury was the speedy messenger of the Roman gods.

orbits the sun every 88 Earth days. That's why the planet is called Mercury. It was named after the speedy messenger of the ancient Roman gods.

100% TIN

Venus, Earth's Sister Planet

Venus is the second closest planet to the sun. Sometimes it is called Earth's twin or sister planet. Venus is the closest planet to Earth, and the two planets are almost the same size.

Venus is surrounded by thick clouds.

If Venus and Earth are twins, they are certainly not identical. Venus is surrounded by thick clouds filled with droplets of acid. If you stood on Venus, you would not be able to see beyond those clouds. And you would be hot. The temperature on Venus is more than 800 degrees Fahrenheit, or more than 425 degrees Celsius.

Venus and Earth travel around the sun in opposite directions. The two planets get as close as 25 million miles, or 40 million kilometers,

800° IN THE SHADE, NOTHING BUT CLOUDS AND ACID RAIN, THIS IS THE LAST TIME WE TAKE A VACATION ON VENUS!

ARF?

apart. They get as far away as 160 million miles, or more than 250 million kilometers.

Seen from Earth, Venus looks very bright because the sun's light is reflected off the clouds. When Venus is traveling away from Earth, it can be seen just before the sun rises in the morning. Years ago, when Venus was seen in the morning, it was called the morning star.

When Venus is moving toward Earth, it can be seen in the evening before the stars come out. At one time Venus was also called the evening star. Now we know that both the morning and the evening stars are Venus.

Mars, the Red Planet

Earth is the third planet from the sun. Mars is the fourth. Since Mars is farther from the sun, it should be colder. It is. The average temperature on Mars is 45 degrees below zero Fahrenheit.

The diameter of Mars is about half that of Earth, and the mass of Mars is also much less than the mass of Earth. Since the mass of Mars

Mars was the Roman god of war.

is less than Earth's, its pull of gravity is less, too. If you weighed 120 pounds, or about 55 kilograms, on Earth, you would weigh 45 pounds, or about 20 kilograms, on Mars.

Mars is tilted on its axis, so it has seasons. It takes Mars about twice as long as it takes Earth to circle the sun, so its seasons are about twice as long as ours.

Mars is covered with dust and rocks containing a reddish mineral. That's why it looks red and is often called the Red Planet. And because it looks red, it was named after the Roman god of war, a warrior who was covered with blood.

Viking I landed on Mars on July 20, 1976.

Thousands of Asteroids

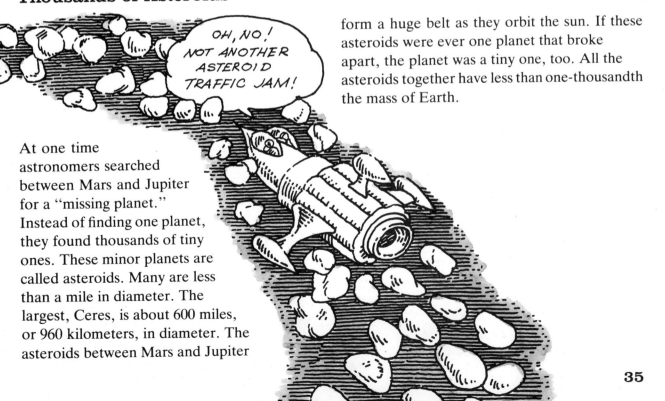

At one time astronomers searched between Mars and Jupiter for a "missing planet." Instead of finding one planet, they found thousands of tiny ones. These minor planets are called asteroids. Many are less than a mile in diameter. The largest, Ceres, is about 600 miles, or 960 kilometers, in diameter. The asteroids between Mars and Jupiter form a huge belt as they orbit the sun. If these asteroids were ever one planet that broke apart, the planet was a tiny one, too. All the asteroids together have less than one-thousandth the mass of Earth.

You Couldn't Live on Jupiter

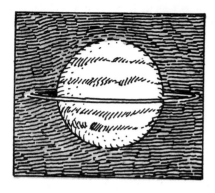

Jupiter is surrounded by a faint ring, similar to Saturn's rings.

The atmosphere on Jupiter is filled with poisonous gas, so you could not live there. You could not stand on Jupiter because it has no solid surface. It is a giant ball of gas. Only toward the center of the ball does the gas become liquid. Much deeper inside Jupiter the gas becomes solid.

But if somehow you were standing on Jupiter, you would be a long way from home. Jupiter never gets closer to Earth than 390 million miles, or some 625 million kilometers, away.

Jupiter is the largest planet in the solar system. If all the other planets were rolled into one large ball, that ball would be smaller than Jupiter. Its diameter is eleven times that of Earth, and its volume is more than one thousand times as great as that of Earth.

Jupiter is not as dense as Earth. But because it is so much bigger, it has more mass and a stronger pull of gravity. Your weight on Jupiter would be 2.65 times your weight on Earth. If your weight on Earth is 100 pounds, or 45 kilograms, on Jupiter you would weigh 265 pounds, or 119 kilograms.

Jupiter has a ring, and scientists have discovered thirteen moons orbiting Jupiter. Some scientists believe there are more.

Jupiter also has a Great Red Spot that covers an area more than three times the size of Earth. The red spot is a storm that has been raging for hundreds of years. The next time you complain because it has rained for several days, imagine what it would be like to live on Jupiter's Red Spot.

Jupiter was named after the king of the Roman gods, because it is the largest of the planets.

Cold Saturn

Saturn is a huge, cold, floating ball of gas. It is the second largest planet in the solar system. Its diameter is about 9½ times the diameter of Earth. But Saturn is not nearly so dense as Earth. If you drop some Earth rocks or soil in water, they will sink. That would not happen with a chunk of Saturn. It would float.

Saturn spins quickly. It spins around its axis in less than eleven hours, so its day is less than

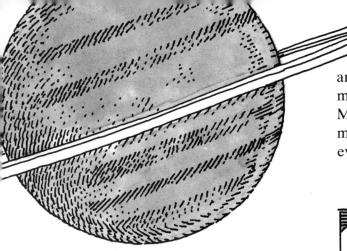

and rock. Saturn also has at least seventeen moons. The largest moon, Titan, is bigger than Mercury. It has its own atmosphere. There may be volcanos, lakes of gas and water, and even primitive life on Titan.

eleven Earth-hours long. But it circles the sun only once every 29½ Earth-years. Someone who is eighty-nine years old on Earth has lived for just three Saturn years.

Thousands of rings circle Saturn's middle. Each ring is made of tiny particles of floating ice

Two Faraway Planets, Uranus and Neptune

Uranus

Neptune

Uranus and Neptune are the seventh and eighth planets from the sun. Both are much bigger than Earth, but they are so far away they can't be seen without a telescope. How far away are they? Well, if you look up at the sky, the moon seems to be a great distance away, and it is. But

Uranus is more than 7,000 times as far from Earth, and Neptune is more than 11,000 times as far away.

You may think that seeing is believing—but scientists knew there was a Neptune even before they saw it. As they watched Uranus, they noticed that something was affecting its orbit. They believed that there must be another planet beyond Uranus. In 1846 they found Neptune very close to where they had predicted it would be.

Uranus was named after the Greek god of the sky, and Neptune was named after the Roman god of the sea.

Pluto, Usually the Ninth Planet

Is Pluto the farthest known planet in the solar system? Usually. Pluto travels in an oval-shaped orbit. Because of the shape of its orbit, at times it is closer to the sun than Neptune is.

Before Pluto was discovered, astronomers had spent twenty-five years looking for it. Something was affecting the orbits of Uranus and Neptune. Only after a new, more powerful telescope was invented, in 1930, could Pluto be found. Some scientists believe that Pluto was not always a planet, that at one time it was Neptune's moon. Pluto is smaller than Earth, but it is so far away that its exact size is not known.

Would life be very different for you if you lived on Pluto? It is very cold there, and you would not be able to breathe the air. But if somehow you did manage to survive on Pluto, you would find out that a year on Pluto is the same as 248 years on Earth. That's a long time between birthdays.

How did Pluto get its name? There was a Greek god named Pluto who ruled the land of the dead. While the planet Pluto may not be the land of the dead, it is certainly a place where no human being could survive.

Pluto was discovered in 1930 at Lowell Observatory in Flagstaff, Arizona.

WHERE IS EACH ROCKET HEADED?

Answers on page 72.

Brain Teasers

1. If three Martians landed on Earth, and the tall, fat green one weighed double the tall, thin green one, and the tall, thin green one weighed triple the short, thin green one, and together they weighed one thousand kilograms, how much did each Martian weigh?

2. If a spaceship to Venus has four doors you can go in and four to go out, and if inside there are three paths you can take and two sets of stairs you can climb, how many different ways can you enter the spaceship?

3. If an astronomer looks through a telescope and sees two planets between two planets, two planets in front of two planets and two planets behind two planets, how many planets does the astronomer see?

4. If you look at all nine planets, you'll see someone eight times. Who is it?

5. If a trip to Saturn would cost $100 for adults, $50 for children under twelve, and $10 for children under four, and if the same number of paying adults, children, and young children were on board and together they paid $800, how many paying passengers would be on board?

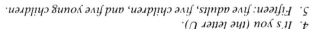
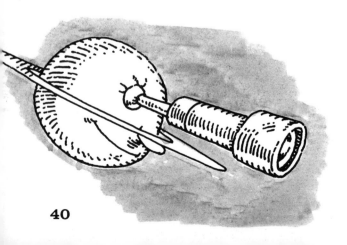

Answers:

1. *The tall fat Martian weighs 600 kilograms. The tall thin Martian weighs 300 kilograms, and the short thin Martian weighs 100 kilograms.*
2. *The spaceship has just four doors, so there are only four ways you can enter.*
3. *Four.*
4. *It's you (the letter U).*
5. *Fifteen: five adults, five children, and five young children.*

40

SCRAMBLED PLANETS

Scrambled below are the names of the planets and other things you might find in outer space. Can you tell what they are?

1. TOPUL
2. UNRSATOAT
3. ROTEME
4. RUSTAN
5. TRIPEJU
6. TILTASELE
7. RAMS
8. HEART
9. PENTUNE
10. MSOCONTUA
11. SUNRAU
12. ERUMCRY
13. TECKOR
14. CAPSCAFRTE

Answers:
1. Pluto
2. Astronaut
3. Meteor
4. Saturn
5. Jupiter
6. Satellite
7. Mars
8. Earth
9. Neptune
10. Cosmonaut
11. Uranus
12. Mercury
13. Rocket
14. Spacecraft

RIDDLES

What's blue, red, and green?
A sad, sunburned Martian.

What's green on the inside and yellow on the outside?
A Martian in a taxicab.

How does a Martian count to fifty-seven?
On its fingers.

What has four legs, a long neck, and lives on Venus?
A lost giraffe.

What have four legs, two wings, and live on Pluto?
Fleas.

How would you telephone Saturn?
Long distance.

What would you need to call Uranus?
A lot of dimes

What is red, white, blue, and green?
A Martian waving an American flag.

What is short, green, and always points north?
A magnetic Martian.

What do you get if you cross a Martian with a cow?
Green milk.

What happens to a Martian when it rains?
He gets wet.

What would you need to call Pluto?
His telephone number.

What's the best way to get to Mercury?
Take the shuttle bus from Venus.

How long would it take to travel to Neptune?
I don't know. It depends on the traffic.

Why don't children on Venus watch television?
They have too much homework.

How would you play tennis on Neptune?
Alone.

Why can't more than one electric Martian
travel in space at a time?
Their cords would get tangled.

What is short, green, and must be plugged in?
An electric Martian.

Don't you just hate it when . . .

. . . your class is taking a trip to Venus
and your parents forgot to sign the
permission slip.

. . . . your space suit is too big and
your mother says you'll grow into it.

. . . you're halfway to Jupiter and
you run out of gas.

. . . you miss the rocket to Saturn because
your mother makes you brush *every* tooth.

. . . your uncle wants to take you to Uranus,
but your father says you have to go to school.

. . . it's cold out and you have to wear
a scarf, mittens, and a sweater over
your space suit.

43

Mars Words

The three words below begin with MARS. Do you know what they are?

1. White, fluffy candy

   _ _ _ _ _ _ - _ _ _ _ _ _

2. Swamp

   _ _ _ _ _

3. Officer of the law

   _ _ _ _ _ _ _

Answers:
1. *Marshmallow.*
2. *Marsh.*
3. *Marshal.*

ASTEROID MAZE

Can you find a path from Mars to Jupiter without touching one of the asteroids?

Answer on page 72.

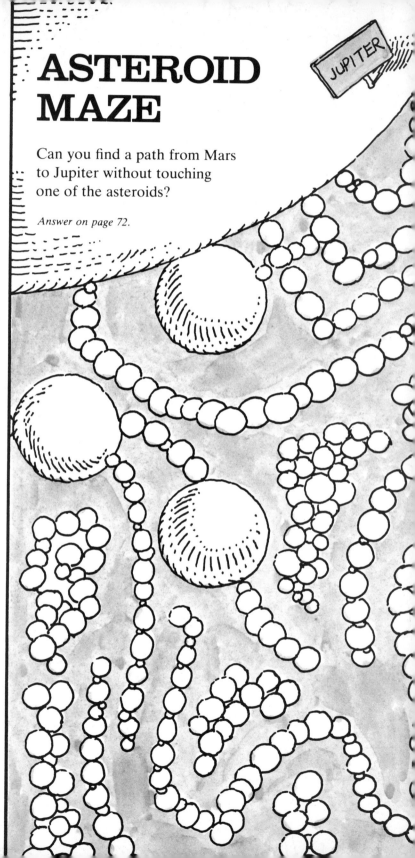

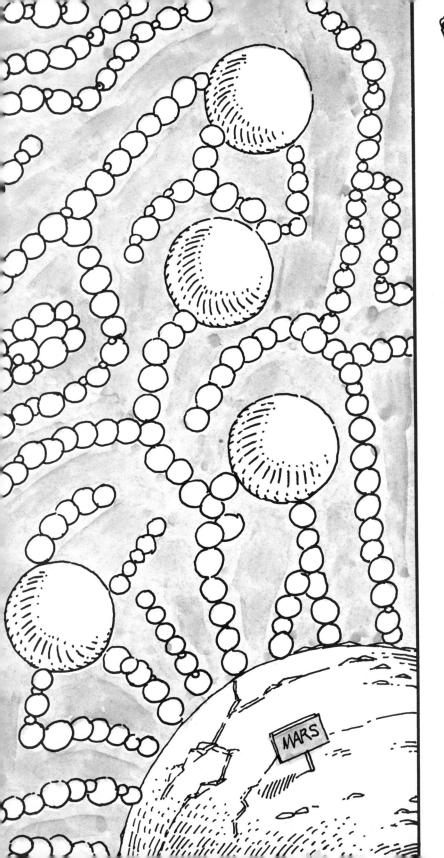

Piggy Astronauts
This little piggy went to Neptune.
This little piggy went to Mars.
This little piggy went to Pluto.
This little piggy went to the moon.
And this little piggy,
The smallest of them all,
Stayed here on Earth
And starts school in the fall.

STARS, BLACK HOLES, U.F.O.s, and MORE

Our own galaxy, the Milky Way

The Milky Way and Other Galaxies

The Milky Way Galaxy is a huge family of stars, dust, and gas that travels together through space. Our sun and the other stars that you can see are only a few of the one hundred billion stars in the galaxy. The Milky Way is flat and round. It is so big that light, which can travel from the sun to Earth in less than nine minutes, would take one hundred thousand years to travel from one end of the Milky Way to the other.

The Milky Way is just one of billions of galaxies in the universe. Three of the galaxies can be seen from Earth without a telescope. But because they are so far away, they look like fuzzy clouds of light.

Galaxies move, and the stars in them move, too. The stars near the center of the galaxy travel faster than those on the outer edges. Each second the sun, which is near the outside edge of the Milky Way, travels more than 150 miles. That's more than 240 kilometers.

All Those Stars

The sun is a star. Like the billions and billions of other stars in the universe, it is a huge ball of glowing gas. But all stars are not the same. They can be white, yellow, blue, or red. The hottest stars, the blue ones, can be up to ten times as hot as some of the other stars. Stars also vary in size. The sun is a medium-sized star.

Some of the very smallest stars, the dwarfs, are even smaller than Earth. The largest stars can be more than three hundred times as big as the sun.

I'M COOL

I'M HOT

I'M VERY AVERAGE

Our sun   *White dwarf*   *Red giant*

LISTEN TO:
THE BLACK HOLE

SIGH...
I USED TO BE A STAR, THEN... THINGS JUST SEEMED TO COLLAPSE.

Nothing Can Escape a Black Hole.

No one has ever seen a black hole. It cannot be seen because nothing can escape a black hole, not even light. Scientists believe that there are many black holes in space. They are formed when a star runs out of fuel and collapses. The bigger a star is the smaller and denser it becomes when it collapses. That small dense "hole" still has all the matter the star had. For its size, it has a huge gravitational pull. Anything that comes close is pulled in and disappears.

It's Not a Bird!
It's Not a Plane!
It's a U.F.O.!

A U.F.O. is an unidentified flying object, something seen in the sky that cannot be explained. U.F.O.s have been reported as cigar-shaped or as balls of light. In 1947 a man reported seeing "saucer-like things" flying about. That's when the term "flying saucer" was first used.

Some reports describe strange creatures in the U.F.O.s. One report said the creatures waved at a group of children. Someone else reported hearing six strange-looking beings in a U.F.O. speaking an unknown language. They lowered a cable, captured a cow, and disappeared with it. During World War Two, Air Force pilots reported seeing "moving lights" flying alongside their planes.

After some investigation many of these U.F.O.s turn out to be meteors, unusual cloud formations, weather balloons, stars, or high flying airplanes.

For twenty-two years the United States Air Force investigated U.F.O.s. After listing and studying more than twelve thousand U.F.O. sightings, the Air Force reported that U.F.O.s

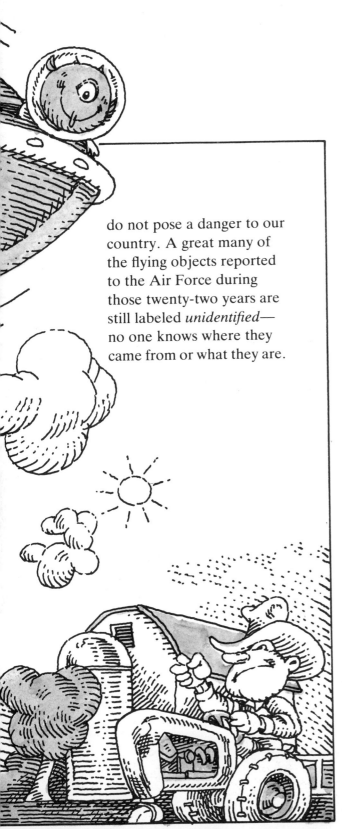

do not pose a danger to our country. A great many of the flying objects reported to the Air Force during those twenty-two years are still labeled *unidentified*—no one knows where they came from or what they are.

Mysteries of Space

Earth is just one of nine planets orbiting the sun. The sun is just one of billions of stars in the Milky Way Galaxy. There are billions of other galaxies in the universe. How big is the universe? Scientists don't really know. They don't even know if the universe has any definite size.

Are there just nine planets in the solar system, or is there another one out there? Pluto was discovered because something was affecting the orbits of Uranus and Neptune. But some

scientists think that Pluto alone is not big enough to account for the effect it is supposed to have on the other planets.

Is there anyone out there? Maybe. With so many billions of stars there's an unknown number of planets. What or who exists on those planets is unknown, too.

Perhaps the biggest mystery is what will be discovered next. As scientists keep working, we keep learning more about the universe we live in.

Meteoroids, Meteors, and Meteorites

Chunks of rock and metal floating in space are called meteoroids. The ones that float near Earth are pulled through our atmosphere by gravity. As they speed toward Earth, they become hot. They glow and form trails of light. These trails of light are called shooting stars, falling stars, or meteors. Most meteors disintegrate before they reach Earth. The ones that do fall to Earth are called meteorites. Millions of meteorites fall to earth each day. Most are tiny, no bigger than a grain of salt. But together, each day, they add more than one thousand tons of rocks and metal to Earth's mass.

1

This chunk of rock and metal, floating in space, is called a meteoroid.

2

The same chunk, falling through Earth's atmosphere, glowing red hot, is now called a meteor.

3

Once the chunk hits the ground, it's called a meteorite.

Here Comes a Comet!

There are thousands of comets in our solar system. The most famous one is Halley's Comet. Every seventy-six years it appears close enough to be seen from Earth.

Comets have a diameter of from six to ten miles. That's ten to sixteen kilometers. They consist of frozen gases, ice, and dust, along with chunks of rock and metal. Comets are mostly in the outer reaches of the solar system, beyond Pluto. At times gravity from one of the planets pulls a comet toward the sun. As it gets closer to the sun, some of its frozen gases melt into vapor, forming a bright tail sometimes millions of miles long.

DON'T BE AFRAID, FOLKS IT'S ONLY HALLEY'S COMET. PS... DUE TO RETURN IN 76 YRS.

IT'S WEIRD! I LIKE IT.

It's Faster Than a Speeding Lightbeam! It's Hyperspace!

Distances in space are measured in light-years. One light-year is the distance light travels through space in one year. How far is that? Light travels 186,000 miles, or almost 300,000 kilometers, in a second. That is about 6 trillion miles, almost 9½ trillion kilometers, in a year. It is hard to imagine anything that can travel that fast. But in science fiction, if you traveled even faster than the speed of light, you would end up in "hyperspace." If you could ever travel that fast, you would be able to race a sunbeam to Earth—and win!

51

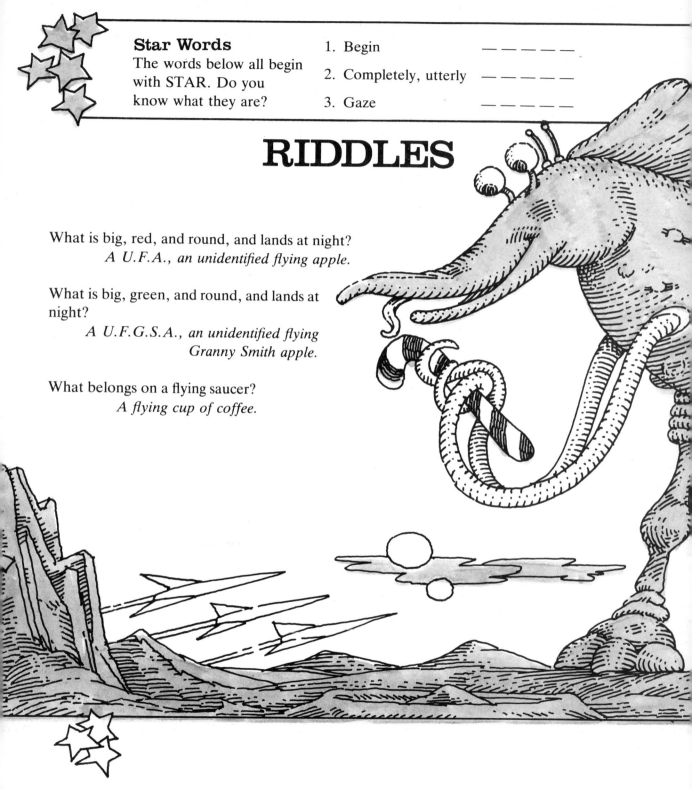

Star Words
The words below all begin with STAR. Do you know what they are?

1. Begin   _ _ _ _ _ _
2. Completely, utterly   _ _ _ _ _ _
3. Gaze   _ _ _ _ _

RIDDLES

What is big, red, and round, and lands at night?
   A U.F.A., an unidentified flying apple.

What is big, green, and round, and lands at night?
   A U.F.G.S.A., an unidentified flying Granny Smith apple.

What belongs on a flying saucer?
   A flying cup of coffee.

4. Surprise   — — — — — — —

5. Very hungry   — — — — — — — —

6. Bird   — — — — — — — —

7. Movie actress   — — — — — — —

8. Carbohydrate   — — — — — —

9. One side of a boat   — — — — — — — — —

What's green and growing?
*A Martian who drinks
plenty of milk.*

What's red, white, and green?
*A Martian eating a peppermint
stick.*

Would you rather be chased by a space
monster or by a fire-eating dragon?
*I'd rather the space monster
chased the dragon.*

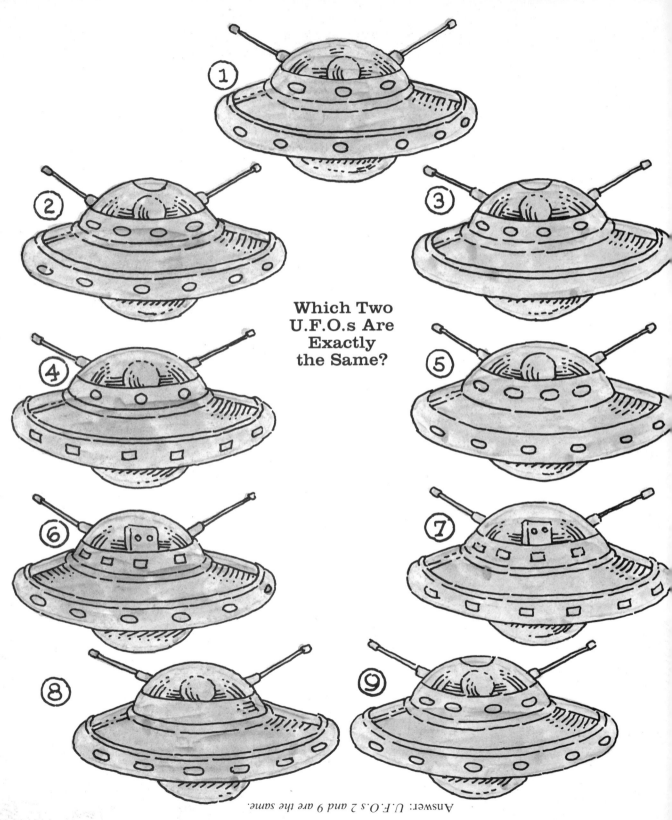

Which Two U.F.O.s Are Exactly the Same?

Answer: U.F.O.s 2 and 9 are the same.

WORD SPLITS

Ten words or word pairs have
been split in three.
Can you put them
together?

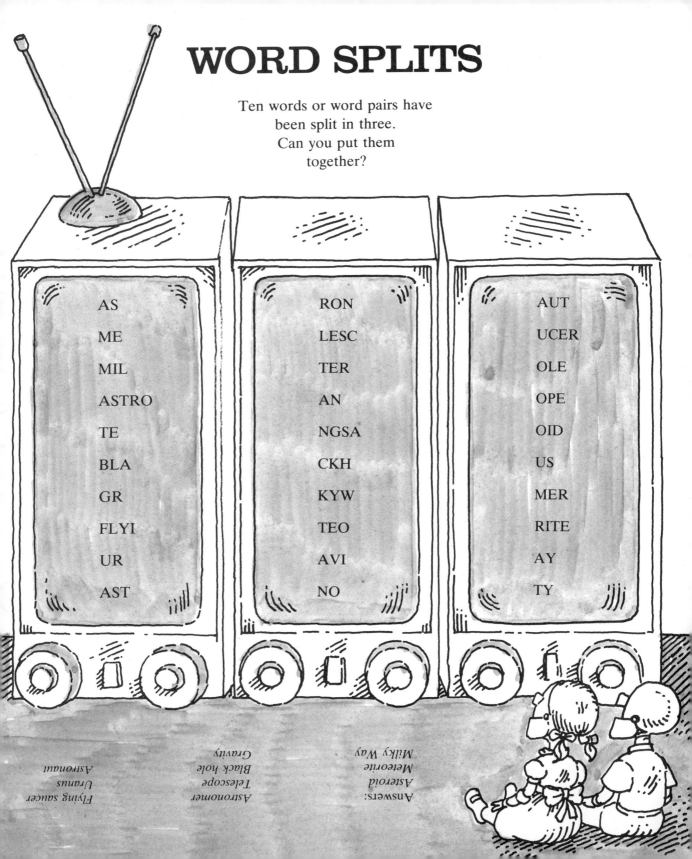

AS	RON	AUT
ME	LESC	UCER
MIL	TER	OLE
ASTRO	AN	OPE
TE	NGSA	OID
BLA	CKH	US
GR	KYW	MER
FLYI	TEO	RITE
UR	AVI	AY
AST	NO	TY

PEOPLE IN SPACE

John H. Glenn, Jr.

First in Space

Yuri A. Gagarin of Russia was the first person in space. He circled Earth once on April 12, 1961.

Alan B. Shepard was the first American in space, but he did not go into orbit. He went up more than 115 miles. That's about 185 kilometers. The whole flight lasted fifteen minutes.

John H. Glenn, Jr., was the first American to circle Earth. He circled it three times. The spacecraft was designed to travel with its widest end forward. Inside, to have room for his legs, John Glenn had to sit facing the narrow end, so he saw where he had been, not where he was going.

Valentina Tereshkova of Russia was the first woman in space. She circled Earth 45 times between June 16 and June 19, 1963. Each time around took 88 minutes.

Edward H. White was the first American to walk in space. He liked it so much outside that after twenty minutes his commander had to tell him to return to the spacecraft.

Neil A. Armstrong was the first person to set foot on the moon—on July 20, 1969. His first words on the moon were, "That's one small step for man, one giant leap for mankind."

Neil A. Armstrong's foot

A walk in space

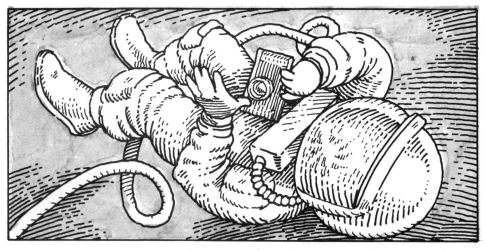

Without gravity you could not pour water into a glass, keep food on a plate, and you could not even sit in a chair unless you were strapped in. Because there is no gravity and things float freely in space, juices and other drinks are dehydrated and kept in closed plastic containers. When astronauts want a drink, they add water from a hose into the container. Then they hold the container up to their mouths and squeeze the drink out. Spaceships are small, so foods are freeze-dried to save space.

In a spacecraft the water in the shower doesn't pour out. It floats around. When the shower is over, the water does not go down a drain. It has to be vacuumed up.

In Skylab, the space station, the astronauts slept in sleeping bags attached to the ceiling. If they had not been attached, the astronauts would have floated around as they slept.

Things and people that are not tied down will float freely.

Living in Space

Living in a traveling spaceship is very different from living on Earth. Everything used in a spaceship must be specially designed.

There is just about no force of gravity at all and no weight in space, so things and people that are not tied down will float freely.

The water in the shower doesn't pour out. It floats around.

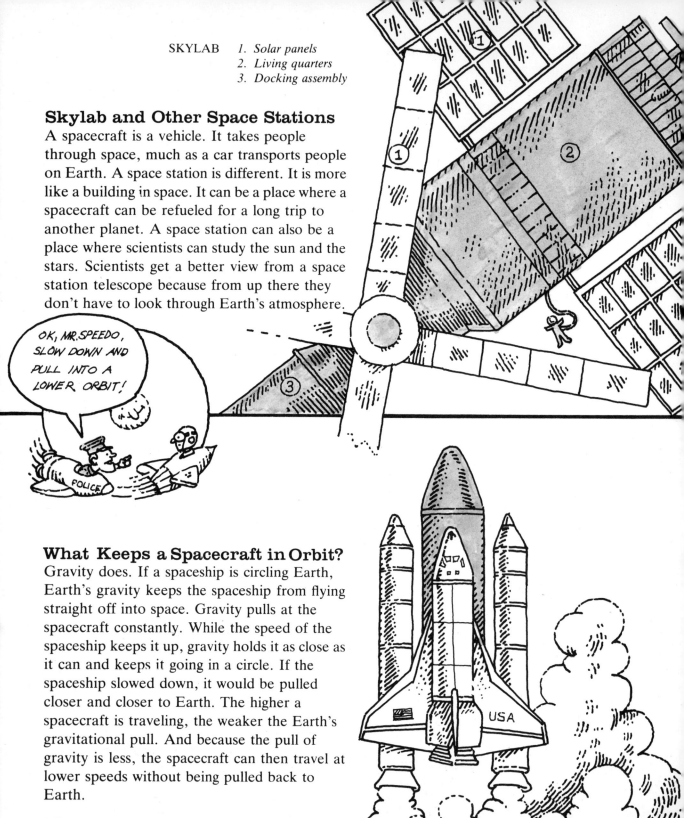

SKYLAB *1. Solar panels*
2. Living quarters
3. Docking assembly

Skylab and Other Space Stations

A spacecraft is a vehicle. It takes people through space, much as a car transports people on Earth. A space station is different. It is more like a building in space. It can be a place where a spacecraft can be refueled for a long trip to another planet. A space station can also be a place where scientists can study the sun and the stars. Scientists get a better view from a space station telescope because from up there they don't have to look through Earth's atmosphere.

What Keeps a Spacecraft in Orbit?

Gravity does. If a spaceship is circling Earth, Earth's gravity keeps the spaceship from flying straight off into space. Gravity pulls at the spacecraft constantly. While the speed of the spaceship keeps it up, gravity holds it as close as it can and keeps it going in a circle. If the spaceship slowed down, it would be pulled closer and closer to Earth. The higher a spacecraft is traveling, the weaker the Earth's gravitational pull. And because the pull of gravity is less, the spacecraft can then travel at lower speeds without being pulled back to Earth.

58

The first space station, Salyut, was sent up by the Russians in 1971. The first space station sent up by the United States was Skylab. It was sent up in 1973. Astronauts went in groups of three and worked in Skylab between May 1973 and February 1974. Sunspots caused less energy to reach Skylab than anticipated, and Skylab began to fall. In 1979 it entered Earth's atmosphere and then fell to Earth. As it fell, it broke into pieces. One large piece landed in Australia. Luckily, no one was hurt.

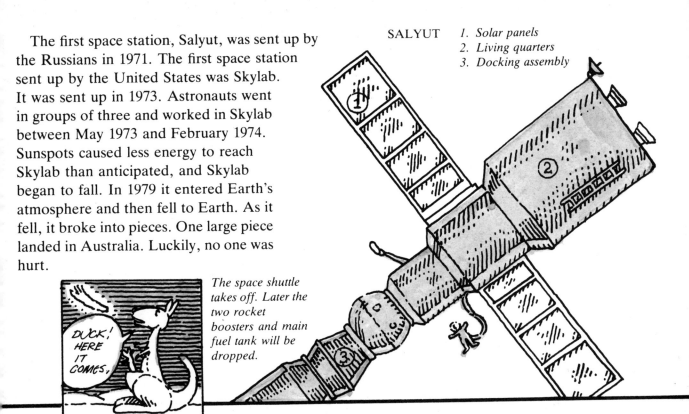

SALYUT
1. *Solar panels*
2. *Living quarters*
3. *Docking assembly*

DUCK! HERE IT COMES.

The space shuttle takes off. Later the two rocket boosters and main fuel tank will be dropped.

Space Shuttles

The earliest spacecraft were designed to make just one flight. A space shuttle is different. It is designed to fly again and again. Space shuttles can carry satellites into space, launch them, repair satellites already in space or even bring them back to Earth. In 1981 the first space shuttle, Columbia, was launched from Cape Canaveral, Florida. Fifty-four hours later it came back and landed in a Southern California desert. Then it was flown back to Cape Canaveral and made ready for its next flight.

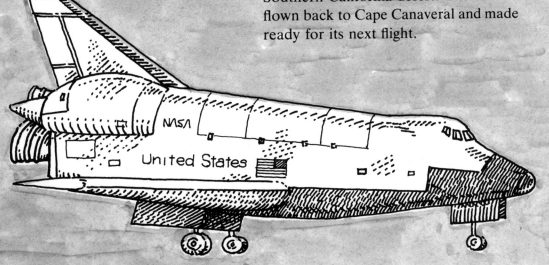

2.

4. HTRAEGNITISIVLLAERAEWEREHSIENOON.

3. When Emma last chuckled, odd Myrna embarrassed Tanya on Mister Allen's rented sloop.

1. JU XBT OJDF PG ZPV UP DPNF.

5.

Of course no astronauts have landed on Mars.
But what if they did and they found these messages?
Would you be able to decipher them?

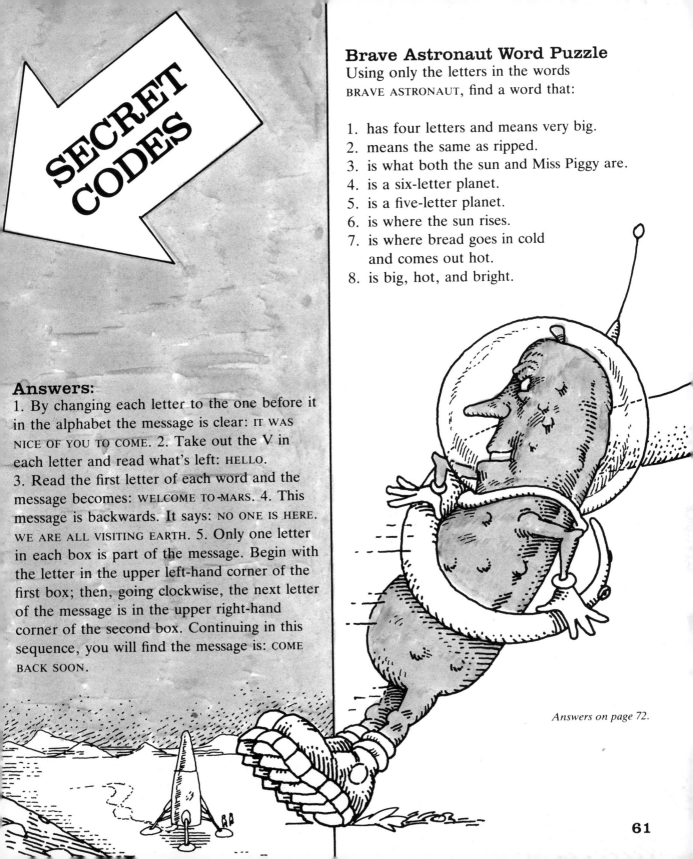

SECRET CODES

Brave Astronaut Word Puzzle

Using only the letters in the words
BRAVE ASTRONAUT, find a word that:

1. has four letters and means very big.
2. means the same as ripped.
3. is what both the sun and Miss Piggy are.
4. is a six-letter planet.
5. is a five-letter planet.
6. is where the sun rises.
7. is where bread goes in cold
   and comes out hot.
8. is big, hot, and bright.

Answers on page 72.

Answers:
1. By changing each letter to the one before it in the alphabet the message is clear: IT WAS NICE OF YOU TO COME. 2. Take out the V in each letter and read what's left: HELLO.
3. Read the first letter of each word and the message becomes: WELCOME TO MARS. 4. This message is backwards. It says: NO ONE IS HERE. WE ARE ALL VISITING EARTH. 5. Only one letter in each box is part of the message. Begin with the letter in the upper left-hand corner of the first box; then, going clockwise, the next letter of the message is in the upper right-hand corner of the second box. Continuing in this sequence, you will find the message is: COME BACK SOON.

What's Next?

Scientists are already talking about factories in space. Because there is no gravity, certain metals, which due to their densities cannot be combined on Earth, can be combined in space to form new alloys. Conditions in space are also ideal for the manufacture of certain medicines.

Soon a power station may be built in space. It would capture energy from the sun and send it back to Earth to be converted into electricity.

Scientists are thinking about traveling to one of the stars. Pioneer 10, a space probe, has already

been sent. A space probe is a spacecraft sent deep into space to gather information. Pioneer carries with it a message of peace and friendship and drawings of a man and a woman to show anyone or anything finding it what Earthlings look like. If it ever does reach a planet orbiting some star other than the sun, it won't be for a long time. It will take Pioneer 10 at least 100,000 years to reach the next closest star.

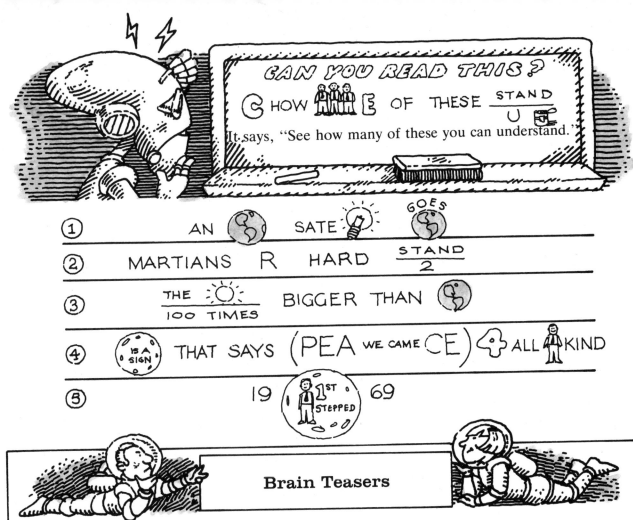

CAN YOU READ THIS?

C HOW 👥👥👥 E OF THESE STAND/U[E]

It says, "See how many of these you can understand."

1. AN 🌍 SATE 💡 GOES🌍

2. MARTIANS R HARD STAND/2

3. THE ☀/100 TIMES BIGGER THAN 🌍

4. (IS A SIGN) THAT SAYS (PEA WE CAME CE) 🌸 ALL 🧍KIND

5. 19 (1ST STEPPED) 69

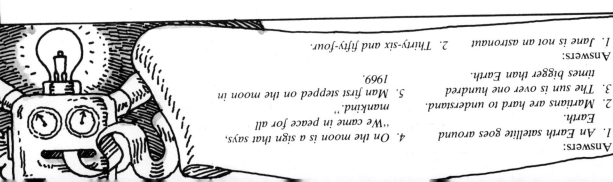

Brain Teasers

1. Two men and two women sat around a card table. Three of them were astronauts. One was not. Read the following statements and see if you can figure out who was not an astronaut.
John sat across from Jack.   Jane and John sat across from astronauts.
June sat next to Jack and John.   June and Jane each sat next to two astronauts.

2. If one half the age of one astronaut equals one third the age of the other and if the difference in their ages is eighteen years, how old is each astronaut?

Answers:
1. *Jane is not an astronaut.*
2. *Thirty-six and fifty-four.*

Answers:
1. *An Earth satellite goes around Earth.*
2. *Martians are hard to understand.*
3. *The sun is over one hundred times bigger than Earth.*
4. *On the moon is a sign that says, "We came in peace for all mankind."*
5. *Man first stepped on the moon in 1969.*

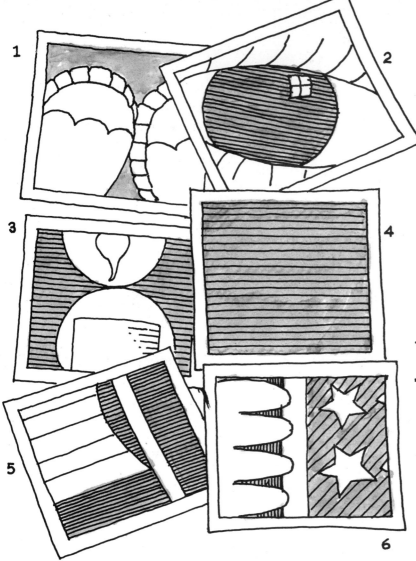

What is red and white
and flies in space?
A peppermint spaceship.

What is green,
wears a helmet, and flies
around and around?
An airsick astronaut.

Photographs from Space

One astronaut wasn't a very good photographer. These are the
photographs he brought back from the moon. Can you tell
what they are?

Answers:
1. *The astronaut's feet.*
2. *The astronaut's eye. He held the camera backwards.*
3. *The lower hemisphere of Earth and the upper hemisphere of another astronaut.*
4. *The astronaut forgot to take off the lens cap.*
5. *Part of the American flag. The astronaut stood too close.*
6. *A close-up of the astronaut holding the American flag.*

RIDDLES

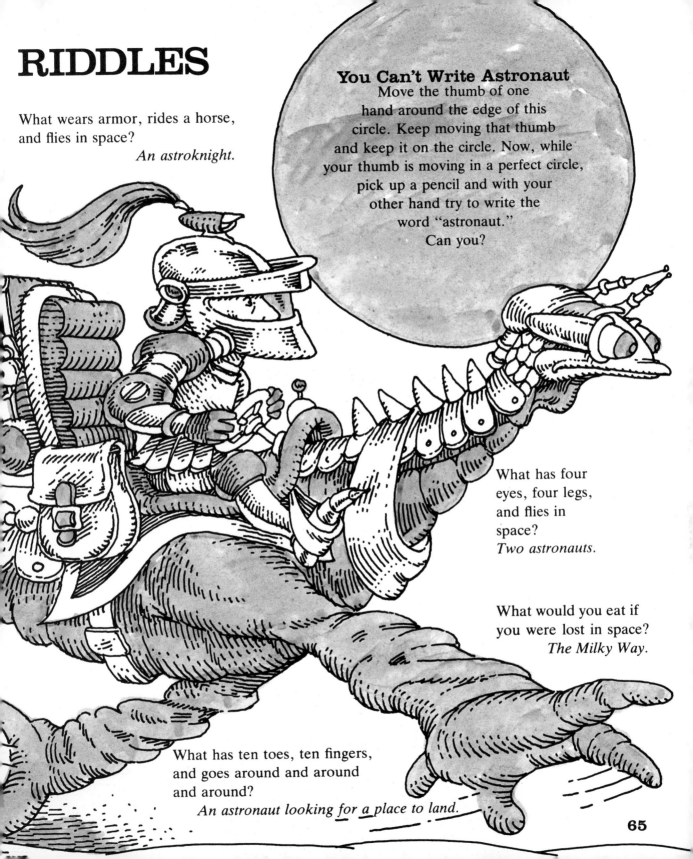

What wears armor, rides a horse, and flies in space?

An astroknight.

You Can't Write Astronaut
Move the thumb of one hand around the edge of this circle. Keep moving that thumb and keep it on the circle. Now, while your thumb is moving in a perfect circle, pick up a pencil and with your other hand try to write the word "astronaut."
Can you?

What has four eyes, four legs, and flies in space?
Two astronauts.

What would you eat if you were lost in space?
The Milky Way.

What has ten toes, ten fingers, and goes around and around and around?
An astronaut looking for a place to land.

65

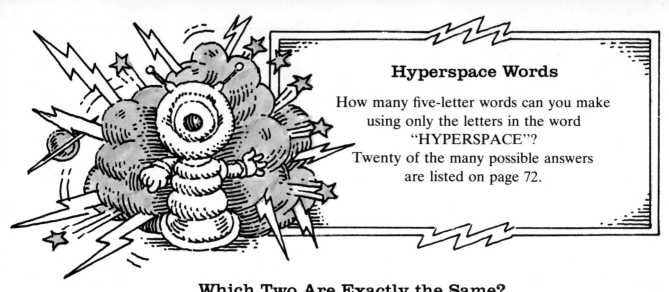

Hyperspace Words

How many five-letter words can you make
using only the letters in the word
"HYPERSPACE"?
Twenty of the many possible answers
are listed on page 72.

Which Two Are Exactly the Same?

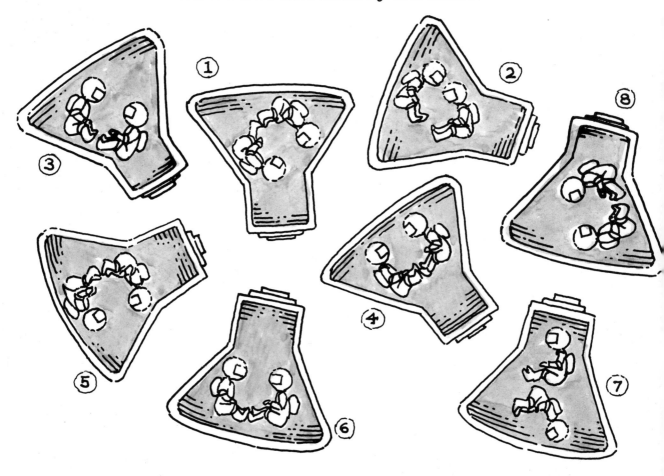

Numbers 3 and 8 are exactly the same.

SPACE COLONY GAME
(a game for 2, 3, or 4 players)

Sometime in the early twenty-first century space colonies may be built. People will get to them by space shuttle. On the colony that will orbit Earth there will be areas for living, farming, and manufacturing.

For the game on the next page, pretend you are going on a space shuttle to visit a space colony. To play, you will need a penny and one moving piece for each player. For moving pieces you can use different-colored buttons, jelly beans, or anything else small.

To see who goes first, each player holds the penny over his head and drops it onto the large circle on page 68. Whatever number the penny lands on, or most of the penny if it lands on two sections, is the number of the first move. The player with the highest number goes first. Then players take turns dropping the penny and moving through space. The first player to make the trip to the space colony and back to Earth is the winner. To complete the trip, you must make a perfect landing—get the exact number you need to land on Earth.

Earth looks like a huge floating ball. Go back 3 spaces for another look.

Watch meteoroids enter Earth's atmosphere. Lose 1 turn.

Weightlessness makes you sick. Lose 1 turn.

1

5

2

4

3

Perfect take-off. Go again.

Shuttle insulating tiles are loose. Go back to Start.

Help load materials onto shuttle. Move ahead 4 spaces.

START

EARTH

SPACE COLONY

Take a side trip to the moon. Go back 6 spaces.

Tour a factory in the space colony. Go ahead 4 spaces.

Stay behind to look at the stars. Lose 1 turn.

Stop to collect moon rocks. Lose 1 turn.

Take a good look at Mars. Move ahead 2 spaces.

Foolishly look for a black hole in space. Lose 2 turns.

69

ANSWERS

Page 7:

There are more than 100 triangles.
Your guess is as good as ours.

Page 9:

Sun numbers 3 and 5 are exactly the same.
Add rays 39, 37, and 24 to total 100.

Page 11:

This is one of the possible answers. Can you
find other paths away from the sun?

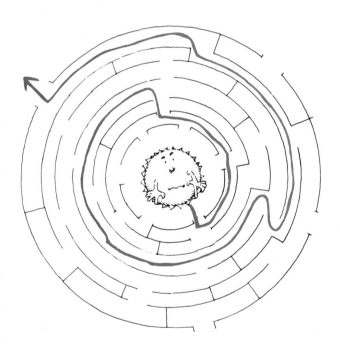

Page 17:

These are two of the possible answers.

Page 18:

1. Joseph came from the United States, Edward
   from Canada, and Nathan from Australia.
2. 667⅓ mph.
3. Two days.
4. The tall man lost four dollars.

Page 29:

Pieces 2 and 7.

Page 39:

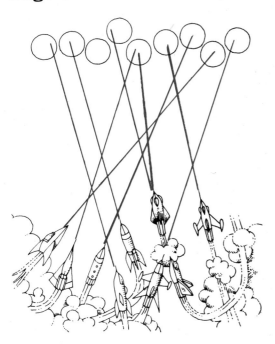

Page 44:

These are two of the possible answers.

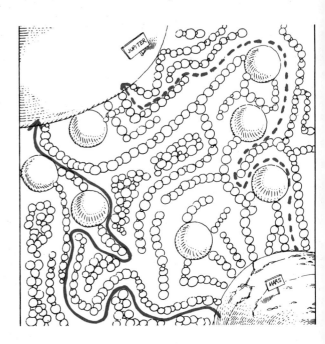

Page 61:

1. *Vast*
2. *Torn*
3. *Star*
4. *Saturn*
5. *Venus*
6. *East*
7. *Toaster*
8. *Sun*

Page 66:

caper	peace
capes	peach
cease	pears
chase	races
crash	reach
erase	sharp
happy	space
harps	spare
paces	spear
parch	spray